ITEM **024 460 260**

D1381391

Wuthering

Artist: Nick Spender

Editor: Jamie Pitman
Editorial Assistant: Mark Williams

Published in Great Britain in 2009 by
Book House, an imprint of
The Salariya Book Company Ltd
25 Marlborough Place, Brighton, BNI IUB
www.salariya.com
www.book-house.co.uk

ISBN-13: 978-1-906370-13-8 (PB)

SALARIYA

A CIP catalogue record for this book is available
from the British Library.

Printed and bound in China.
Printed on paper from sustainable sources.

Visit our website at **www.salariya.com**
for **free** electronic versions of:
You Wouldn't Want to be an Egyptian Mummy!
You Wouldn't Want to be a Roman Gladiator!
Avoid Joining Shackleton's Polar Expedition!
Avoid Sailing on a 19th-Century Whaling Ship!

Picture credits:
p. 42: TopFoto.co.uk
p. 45: iStockphoto

Every effort has been made to trace copyright holders. The Salariya Book Company apologises for any omissions and would be
pleased, in such cases, to add an acknowledgement in future editions.

Wuthering Heights

Emily Brontë

Illustrated by

Nick Spender

Retold by

Jim Pipe

Series created and designed by

David Salariya

'May you not rest,
as long as I am living.
You said I killed you –
haunt me then.'

CHARACTERS

(for more detail, see the Family Tree on page 44)

Heathcliff

Catherine (Cathy)
Earnshaw

Edgar Linton

Isabella Linton,
sister of Edgar

Mr Lockwood, current
tenant of Thrushcross
Grange

Nelly Dean,
housekeeper of
Thrushcross Grange

Hindley Earnshaw,
brother of Catherine Earnshaw

Mr Earnshaw,
father of Catherine and
Hindley Earnshaw

Hareton Earnshaw,
son of Hindley

Catherine Linton,
daughter of Edgar and Catherine

Linton Heathcliff,
son of Heathcliff
and Isabella

THE MYSTERIOUS LANDLORD

It is the winter of 1801. Mr Lockwood is settling into his new home at Thrushcross Grange on the Yorkshire moors.[2] He moved to this bleak, lonely place after a failed love affair.

Lockwood crosses the moors to visit his landlord, the dark and mysterious Heathcliff.

Heathcliff invites Lockwood into his manor, Wuthering[3] Heights. An inscription[4] over the door reads 'Hareton Earnshaw, 1500'.

I wonder what the history of this place is?

Once inside, Heathcliff vanishes. Lockwood is left alone with a group of fierce, snarling dogs. He has to defend himself with a poker!

Lockwood cries out for help. Shortly after, Heathcliff's housekeeper, Zillah, rushes into the room and beats the dogs off with her frying pan.

Hearing the dogs barking, Heathcliff storms in. Lockwood is mad at him, but he calms down when his host offers him a glass of wine.

The two men discuss life on the moors. Heathcliff seems at home in this wild, lonely place. Lockwood plans to visit again the next day.

1. tenant: a person who rents a property.
2. Yorkshire: a county in the north of England.
3. wuthering: a Yorkshire word meaning stormy and windy.
4. inscription: letters or words carved on wood, stone or metal.

STRANDED!

> I will get in!

> Follow me...

A few days later, Lockwood makes the four-mile walk to Wuthering Heights. As he approaches, snow begins to fall. He notices the gate is chained so he jumps over and runs up to the front door.

Lockwood knocks until his knuckles tingle, but no-one lets him in. Suddenly, a young man appears behind him.

> Ah, so this is Heathcliff's 'missis'!

> Were you asked to tea?

> No, but I should like a cup!

The young man takes a winding route around the back of the house. Eventually, Lockwood is led into a warm sitting room. Here he finds a roaring fire – and a beautiful girl.

Lockwood tries to chat politely, but the girl is rude and unfriendly – just like Heathcliff. All the while, the young man stares angrily at the two of them from the other side of the room.

> Lockwood, what are you doing out in this snowstorm?

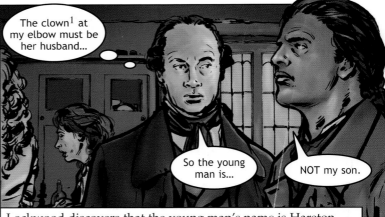

> The clown[1] at my elbow must be her husband...

> So the young man is...

> NOT my son.

When Heathcliff arrives, he is surprised to see Lockwood. He says that the girl is Catherine, his daughter-in-law.

Lockwood discovers that the young man's name is Hareton Earnshaw – the same name that was above the door!

1. clown: country bumpkin.

I don't think I can get home without a guide.

Take the road you came.

After dinner, Lockwood looks out of the window. The snow is falling hard and the light is fading. Lockwood fears that the roads will soon be buried by snow and he won't be able to find his way back to Thrushcross Grange.

Instead of helping him, the others talk amongst themselves. Seething with rage, Lockwood stomps out into the night.

I'll return the lantern in the morning.

Lockwood borrows a lantern. Heathcliff's servant thinks he is trying to steal it, and sets the dogs on him.

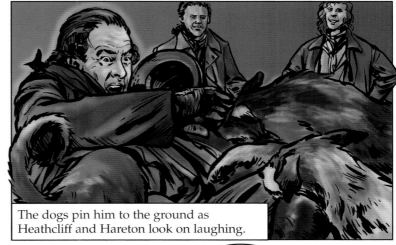

The dogs pin him to the ground as Heathcliff and Hareton look on laughing.

Come in, and I'll cure it.

Shhh! Don't make a sound and put out that candle.

Why?

My master never lets anyone lodge here willingly.

By the time Heathcliff calls off the dogs, Lockwood feels dizzy and faint, and his nose is bleeding. When the housekeeper, Zillah, comes out to see what has happened, she takes pity on Lockwood.

Zillah offers Lockwood a glass of brandy, then shows him upstairs. She warns him that the room is usually out of bounds as Heathcliff has a strange feeling about it.

THE FACE AT THE WINDOW

Tired and confused, Lockwood shuts the door and climbs into bed. The bed has doors like a cupboard. It also sits next to a window so that the window ledge is like a bedside table.

As he puts his candle down, Lockwood sees that someone has scratched three names again and again into the ledge: Catherine Earnshaw, Catherine Linton and Catherine Heathcliff.

When his candle accidentally burns one of the books on the ledge, Lockwood finds a diary written 25 years before by a Cathy Earnshaw.

In the diary, Cathy describes a rainy day at Wuthering Heights just after her father died. She and her playmate Heathcliff were horribly bullied by her mean older brother, Hindley. As he reads, Lockwood becomes drowsy. Soon, he is fast asleep.

Lockwood has a nightmare about a preacher leading an angry mob. Then a loud tapping sound wakes him.

It is a fir cone tapping on the window. He tries to snap off the branch, but forgetting the window is closed, he smashes the glass.

A little, ice-cold hand grabs his wrist and a voice speaks from the darkness. Lockwood sees a child's face peering through the window.

Let me go, if you want me to let you in.

Begone. I'll never let you in, not if you beg for 20 years!

In terror, Lockwood tries to free his hand by rubbing the ghostly figure's wrist on the broken glass.

Who showed you up to this room?

Heathcliff bursts in.

I should throw you out!

This place is haunted!

Heathcliff is in a mad rage but when Lockwood explains what has happened, he calms down.

Come in! Come in, Cathy, once more!

As Lockwood heads downstairs to the kitchen, he hears Heathcliff crying out.

At your idle tricks[1] again?

I'll do what I please!

Things are no calmer the following day. Lockwood interrupts a bitter argument between Heathcliff and his daughter-in-law, Catherine.

Lockwood can't get away quickly enough. However, he accepts Heathcliff's offer to guide him home. It takes four hours to walk back through the thick snow. When Lockwood finally arrives back at Thrushcross Grange, he is exhausted.

1. At your idle tricks: being lazy; playing games.

NELLY BEGINS HER STORY

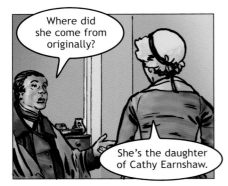

Where did she come from originally?

She's the daughter of Cathy Earnshaw.

That evening, feeling weak and ill, Lockwood asks Nelly Dean, his housekeeper, to tell him about the young girl at Wuthering Heights.

I nursed her, the poor thing!

Nelly explains that young Catherine was once married to wealthy Mr Heathcliff's son, Linton.

Catherine is the last Linton and Hareton is the last Earnshaw.

Catherine is Hareton's cousin, and the daughter of Cathy Earnshaw, whose father used to own Wuthering Heights.

I could not leave him to starve.

I grew up as a servant at Wuthering Heights, alongside Cathy, and her brother Hindley...

While Cathy and Hindley were still children, their father, Mr Earnshaw, went on a trip to Liverpool[1]...

He returned with a ragged child he'd found living on the streets. The Earnshaws named him Heathcliff.

Come and play, Heathcliff!

Heathcliff is brought up as a member of the Earnshaw family. Cathy and Hindley resent Heathcliff at first, but in time Cathy and Heathcliff become as thick as thieves.[2]

You just want to wheedle[3] my father out of all he has.

Mr Earnshaw is very fond of Heathcliff, but Hindley bullies him. During an argument between the two boys, Hindley throws a heavy iron weight at Heathcliff, hitting him on the chest.

1. Liverpool: a major seaport in the north-west of England.
2. thick as thieves: very good friends who share everything.
3. wheedle: to cheat or influence someone by flattering them.

A short time later, Mr Earnshaw's wife dies and he too falls ill. He has decided to send Hindley to college.

He's dead, Heathcliff, he's dead!

One night, three years later, Cathy finds her father dead. Hindley, now 17, returns home for the funeral.

No more lessons! You can work in the fields.

Hindley brings home his new wife, Frances. Now that he is master of the house, he takes his revenge on Heathcliff.

Bolt the doors. No-one shall let them in!

However, Cathy and Heathcliff still find time to go off onto the moors together to play. When Hindley finds out, he is furious.

Where is young Cathy?

Despite Hindley's orders, Nelly waits for them, and is shocked when only Heathcliff returns, soaked to the skin.

Idiots! Arguing over who should hold the puppy!

Now she's rolling around the ground crying!

Heathcliff explains that they went to Thrushcross Grange to spy on Edgar and Isabella, the spoilt children of the Lintons.

Skulker, the Lintons' bulldog, heard them laughing and bit Cathy. Heathcliff tried to free her.

You wicked boy!

Cathy was carried inside Thrushcross Grange, but Heathcliff was thrown out for swearing at Mr Linton.

One word to Cathy and that's it.

Hindley is angry when he hears what has happened. He forbids Heathcliff from ever seeing Cathy again.

THE LINTONS

"Those curls really suit you, dear."

Cathy stays at the Grange for five weeks to recover from her attack. Mrs Linton does her best to rid Cathy of her wild ways.

"Is Heathcliff not here?"

She returns to Wuthering Heights, transformed into a young lady. She does not know Heathcliff has been banned from talking to her.

"Heathcliff, you may welcome Cathy like the other servants."

Hindley enjoys mocking Heathcliff.

"I shall be as dirty as I please!"

Cathy teases Heathcliff for being dirty.

"Let me dress you smart for Miss Cathy."

The next day, the Lintons are invited to a Christmas party at Wuthering Heights. Nelly helps Heathcliff get ready.

"Lock him in the garret[1] until dinner is over."

But Mrs Linton wants Heathcliff kept away from her children, Edgar and Isabella. So Hindley's servant is ordered to take Heathcliff upstairs.

As Heathcliff is leaving, Edgar makes fun of his long hair. Heathcliff angrily smashes a bowl of hot apple sauce in Edgar's face.

"Why did you speak to him, Edgar? Now he'll be flogged.[2]"

Cathy is angry.

After dinner, Cathy sneaks up to see Heathcliff. She climbs into the garret through a skylight on the roof and keeps Heathcliff company.

1. garret: an attic or loft.
2. flogged: whipped.

I don't care how long I wait, if I can only do it.

Mrs Dean, do sit still another half an hour!

Well, several months later, Hindley's wife Frances gave birth to a boy, Hareton...

...but she died soon after, so I brought up the baby.

Later, Nelly takes Heathcliff to the kitchen for some supper. Heathcliff tells her that he will get his revenge on Hindley.

By this point in Nelly Dean's story, it is getting late and Nelly is ready to go to bed. But Mr Lockwood persuades her to carry on.

Hurry up, you idiot!

Good day, Miss Cathy.

Why have you that silk frock on? Nobody coming here?

Edgar and Isabella Linton may call in.

Hindley starts drinking heavily. He takes out his sorrows on his servants, especially Heathcliff. Meanwhile, his sister Cathy is spending more and more time with Edgar Linton.

With Heathcliff, Cathy is the same wild child she always was. One afternoon, when Hindley is away, Heathcliff asks her to spend some time with him.

Don't turn me out[1] for those silly friends of yours.

Why should I be with you? You might as well be a baby for anything you say to amuse me.

I'm not come too soon, am I?

Heathcliff is hurt by Cathy's cruel words. Just then, Edgar enters – without his sister Isabella – and Heathcliff storms off.

1. turn me out: send me away.

LITTLE HARETON

What are you doing there, Nelly?

My work, miss.

Cathy wants to be alone with Edgar, but Nelly has orders from Hindley to watch her.

Take yourself and your dusters off!

Cathy works herself into a fury and pinches and slaps Nelly. When little Hareton begins to cry, Cathy shakes him.

You've made me afraid and ashamed of you! I'll not come again.

When Edgar tries to stop Cathy from hurting the child, she slaps him. Shocked, he turns and leaves.

Edgar catches a last glimpse of Cathy through the window and decides to come back inside. Nelly sees that he loves Cathy.

Later...

Kiss me or I'll break your neck!

After Cathy and Edgar have gone upstairs, Hindley arrives home, drunk and in a terrible rage. Nelly goes to hide little Hareton but Hindley rushes in and grabs the boy.

On his way up the stairs, Hindley stumbles...

Hareton falls...

But Heathcliff is there to catch him.

It's a pity Hindley can't kill himself with drink.

Will you keep a secret for me?

It would degrade[1] me to marry Heathcliff. Hindley has brought him down so low.

Later...

If he had only stayed...

He would have heard Cathy say that she loved him more deeply than anything else in the world...

Nelly is in the kitchen rocking Hareton on her knee, when Cathy reveals that Edgar has asked her to marry him.

Unknown to the two women, Heathcliff is listening. He can bear no more and leaves in a rage of despair.

If Heathcliff and I married, we should be beggars. If I marry Edgar, I can help him... I *am* Heathcliff – he's always, always on my mind.

That night, Heathcliff runs away from Wuthering Heights. Cathy spends the night outdoors in a storm, searching for him. She catches a terrible fever, and is soon close to dying. The Lintons take Cathy to Thrushcross Grange to recover.

Three years later...

Though Cathy gets better, Mr and Mrs Linton catch the fever and die within a few days of each other.

No-one knows where Heathcliff has gone. Cathy and Edgar finally marry, and Nelly goes to live in the Grange with them.

Hareton is left at Wuthering Heights with his drunken father Hindley and a bad-tempered servant.

1. degrade: take down or lower.

HEATHCLIFF'S RETURN

Nelly again stops her story, glancing at the clock over the chimney. To their astonishment, it's half past one. Lockwood finally allows her to go to bed.

Lockwood remains ill for the next four weeks. Heathcliff pays him a brief visit.

Nelly continues her tale.

In the months following Cathy and Edgar Linton's marriage, they seem very happy, though Edgar is afraid of Cathy's moods.

Then, one evening in September, Nelly hears a deep voice, strange yet familiar. It's Heathcliff! After being away for three years, the rough boy has grown into a tall, handsome gentleman. Nelly hardly recognises him.

Cathy is overjoyed…

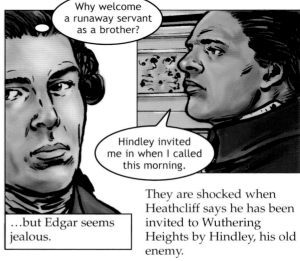

…but Edgar seems jealous.

They are shocked when Heathcliff says he has been invited to Wuthering Heights by Hindley, his old enemy.

Will you walk with us, Heathcliff?

Of course!

Nelly explains that earlier in the day, Hindley was dazzled by the large sums of money Heathcliff was gambling in a card game.

Cathy and Isabella, Edgar's sister, begin to make regular visits to Wuthering Heights. In return, Heathcliff visits them at the Grange. Heathcliff seems like a new man – but Nelly suspects he still wants revenge on Hindley.

I wouldn't be you for a kingdom! He's a fierce, pitiless, wolfish man.

For shame! You poisonous friend!

Isabella begins to fall in love with Heathcliff, who encourages her, despite still being in love with Cathy. When Cathy finds out, she tries to warn Isabella about Heathcliff.

Nelly watches Heathcliff closely.

He's like an evil beast waiting his time to spring and destroy.

Hareton, it's Nelly, your nurse!

Damn you!

It's that goblin Heathcliff!

When Nelly goes to talk to Hindley at Wuthering Heights, Hareton, now aged six, throws stones at her.

Heathcliff, still bitter about Hindley's past behaviour, has taught Hareton to call his father 'Devil Daddy'.

Heathcliff has turned Hareton into a rough little boy. Nelly wins him over by giving him an orange, but when Heathcliff suddenly appears, she runs back to the Grange in terror.

CATHY CONFRONTS HEATHCLIFF

The next day, at the Grange, Nelly spots Heathcliff kissing Isabella. She tells Cathy what she has seen.

In the kitchen, Cathy orders Heathcliff to reveal his true feelings about Isabella.

When Edgar hears from Nelly what is going on, he storms into the kitchen and bans Heathcliff from further visits to the house.

However, Cathy locks them all inside the kitchen and throws the key away, forcing Edgar to face Heathcliff alone.

Edgar is terrified but, shamed by Cathy's insults, he springs forward and punches Heathcliff, before managing to escape to get help.

Realising he cannot fight off Edgar's servants, Heathcliff smashes the door's lock with a poker and flees.

1. brace: a pair.

When Edgar returns to the room, he is furious with Cathy, but she refuses to speak to him. Later, when Nelly answers her call, she sees Cathy sobbing on the sofa and grinding her teeth in rage.

That night, Cathy locks herself in her bedroom and refuses to eat for the next two days. Edgar goes to his library and ignores her.

Edgar warns Isabella that if she pursues Heathcliff, he will cast her out of the Linton family forever.

Finally, Cathy allows Nelly to bring her some porridge to eat. Nelly is shocked when Cathy starts talking wildly.

Cathy staggers to the window and forces it open. Though it is night, she thinks she can see Wuthering Heights.

1. insane: mad.
2. venture: dare to come.

AN UNHAPPY MARRIAGE

Just then, Edgar enters Cathy's bedroom. He is shocked to find Cathy so weak, and orders Nelly to fetch Dr Kenneth. The doctor is confident that Cathy will recover.

Talking to Nelly, Dr Kenneth reveals that earlier that night, a friend of his saw Heathcliff persuading Isabella to run away and marry him.

When he finds out, Edgar can't believe that Isabella has gone with Heathcliff. He now wants nothing to do with her.

For two months, Edgar and Nelly nurse Cathy through her illness. They learn she is pregnant. Meanwhile, Isabella writes to Edgar asking him to forgive her.

When Edgar ignores her letter, Isabella writes to Nelly in desperation.

Isabella tells how Hareton and Hindley treat her terribly, even threatening to set the dogs on her.

Since their marriage, Heathcliff has turned into a devil. Isabella realises that being cruel to her is his way of punishing Edgar for making Cathy ill.

Though Hindley hates Heathcliff, he is no friend to Isabella. He is too busy plotting to kill Heathcliff.

22   1. She went of her own accord: Isabella went willingly.

I don't care if you tell him...

...put him on his guard, and watch for him.

You may call at Wuthering Heights, if you like, and say that I'm sorry to have lost her.

Hindley takes delight in showing Isabella the weapon he will use to kill Heathcliff – a pistol with a knife attached to its barrel. Isabella is convinced that Hindley has gone mad.

Realising she's made a terrible mistake, Isabella begs Nelly to visit her at Wuthering Heights. Nelly tells Edgar about the letter, but he refuses to see his sister or write to her.

Before you leave, promise that you'll get me an interview between us. I *will* see her!

When Nelly arrives at Wuthering Heights, she sees Isabella hiding upstairs. But before she gets a chance to speak to her, Heathcliff sees her and demands to hear about Cathy. He asks if he may come to visit her.

You must not — you shall never — return through my means.

In that case, you'll not leave Wuthering Heights!

Heathcliff threatens Nelly, then thrusts a letter into her hands.

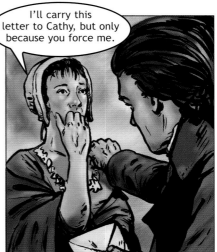

I'll carry this letter to Cathy, but only because you force me.

A Sad End

Four days later, while Edgar is at church, Nelly hands Heathcliff's letter to Cathy. Cathy is now so weak, she can't even hold the letter, so she asks Nelly to read it out to her.

Nelly is about to tell Cathy who the letter is from when Heathcliff himself strides into the room. He grasps Cathy in his arms.

They hear the bells of the church ringing out. Edgar will be home soon.

As she hears Edgar coming up the stairs, Nelly screams, and Cathy collapses into Heathcliff's arms.

1. fiend: devil.

Heathcliff forces Cathy's frail form into Edgar's arms as he enters the room. Nelly pushes Heathcliff out, promising to send him word about Cathy in the morning.

Heathcliff waits outside in the garden so he can be near to Cathy. At around 12 o'clock that night, Cathy gives birth to a daughter, Catherine. Two hours later, Cathy is dead. Edgar is devastated.

When Nelly goes into the garden to tell Heathcliff, she finds him leaning against an old ash tree. He seems to know already that Cathy is dead.

Heathcliff curses Cathy for the torment[1] she has caused him. In a sad fury, he dashes his head against the tree trunk and howls like a wild animal.

The grieving Edgar stays by Cathy's body day and night until the funeral. But when he leaves for an hour to get some sleep, Nelly lets Heathcliff in to see Cathy one last time.

Later, Nelly discovers that Heathcliff has opened the locket[2] around Cathy's neck and replaced a lock of Edgar's hair with a lock of his own.

Nelly twists Edgar's lock around Heathcliff's, and leaves them both in the locket together.

1. torment: suffering, pain.
2. locket: a small, hinged case, which opens up to reveal a portrait or other personal item.

THE FIGHT

Though invited to the funeral, Cathy's brother Hindley does not come. Edgar refuses to invite his sister, Isabella. To everyone's surprise, Cathy is not buried in the Linton tomb, nor by the graves of her family.

Instead, Edgar asks that Cathy be buried in a corner of the churchyard so that she may overlook the moors that she so loved so much.

I've run all the way — I can't count the number of falls I've had.

Nelly tells Lockwood that Edgar now lies in the same spot on the moors, buried beside Cathy.

The day after Cathy's funeral, Isabella arrives at the Grange, hair dripping with rain and snow, her face scratched and bruised.

Isabella says Hindley wanted to go to Cathy's funeral, but could not bear to go. Instead, he began drinking heavily.

Damn that hellish villain!

He knocks at the door as if he were master already![1]

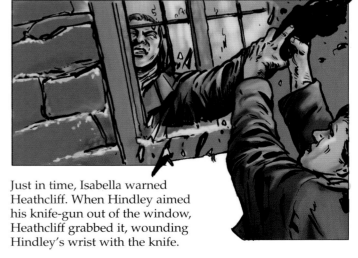

When Heathcliff went to visit Cathy's grave, Hindley locked him out of the house. He told Isabella that he planned to shoot Heathcliff.

Just in time, Isabella warned Heathcliff. When Hindley aimed his knife-gun out of the window, Heathcliff grabbed it, wounding Hindley's wrist with the knife.

---

1. as if he were master already: Hindley knows that Heathcliff plans to take control of Wuthering Heights once Hindley is dead. Heathcliff now knocks on the door as if it were already his property.

Heathcliff broke in…

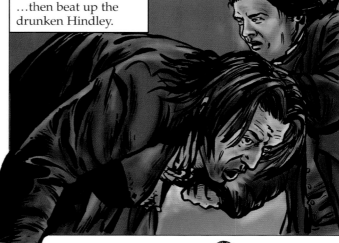

…then beat up the drunken Hindley.

Get out, Isabella, before I stamp you to death!

God give me strength to strangle him!

When he woke the next morning, Hindley could not remember why he felt so sore. After Isabella told him, an almighty row broke out between Isabella, Hindley and Heathcliff.

Heathcliff threw a knife, just missing Isabella. As she ran out, the men started fighting again.

I'd rather hell than another night at Wuthering Heights!

Finally, Isabella crossed the moors to the Grange, to escape from the madness at Wuthering Heights.

Mother!

Finishing her story, Isabella says goodbye to Nelly and leaves for London. A few months later, she gives birth to Heathcliff's son, Linton. Over the next twelve years, she keeps in touch with Nelly.

Though Heathcliff later discovers where Isabella is, he never goes to visit. In fact, he never sees his wife again. When Linton is 12 years old, Isabella dies of a fever.

THE COUSINS MEET

Meanwhile, at the Grange...

Poor lad — Hindley was just twenty-seven.

Six months after Cathy's death, Hindley dies. Nelly goes to Wuthering Heights to organise the funeral, and to bring Hindley's son Hareton back to Thrushcross Grange. On the way, she meets Dr Kenneth.

Dr Kenneth tells her that Hindley died without a penny. Heathcliff, who had lent Hindley large amounts of money to gamble with, is now the owner of Wuthering Heights.

That fool's body should be buried at the crossroads![1]

Poor Hareton has to live with his father's enemy!

12 years later...

If I can't have my way, Nelly, I'll tell papa!

Heathcliff is happy to see Hindley dead, but he refuses to allow Nelly to take Hareton to the Grange. He plans to bring the boy up himself.

Nelly is sad to see that Hareton, who should have inherited Wuthering Heights, is forced to work for Heathcliff instead.

Nelly enjoys bringing up Cathy's baby. But at 13, young Catherine Linton is clever and strong-willed.

Now, am I old enough to go to Penistone Crags?[2]

That road runs close by Wuthering Heights.

Not yet, love, not yet.

Edgar, remembering the past, bans his daughter from going to the moors on her own, so she knows nothing of Wuthering Heights, Heathcliff, or her cousin Hareton.

1. buried at the crossroads: buried like a criminal, not deserving to be buried in sacred ground.
2. Penistone Crags: a fictional rock formation on the moors, supposedly containing a 'Fairy Cave'. It is probably based on Ponden Kirk, near Emily Brontë's home in Haworth.

A few days later, when Edgar hears from Isabella that she is dying, he rushes to London to take care of his nephew, young Linton.

Edgar is away for three weeks. One day, Catherine tricks Nelly into letting her go for a ride. Trotting off on her pony, she heads for Penistone Crags. When Catherine does not return for tea, Nelly runs after her across the moors.

Exhausted, Nelly finally reaches Wuthering Heights. Here she finds Catherine and Hareton happily chatting away. Though secretly glad at finding Catherine safe and well, Nelly angrily orders her back to Thrushcross Grange.

To persuade her to go, Nelly tells Catherine that Hareton is just a servant.

Hearing this, Catherine orders Hareton to get her horse for her. Hareton is furious.

When Nelly explains that Hareton is her cousin, Catherine is horrified.

Catherine promises not to tell Edgar about the visit. Nelly fears Edgar will sack[1] her if he finds out.

1. sack her: fire her from her job.

LINTON COMES HOME

After Isabella's death, Edgar brings Heathcliff's and Isabella's son, Linton, back from London to the Grange. Catherine is disappointed to find her cousin is frail and weak.

That evening, Heathcliff's servant turns up at the Grange. Heathcliff wants his son, Linton, to come to Wuthering Heights. Edgar reluctantly promises to send Linton the next day.

Edgar asks Nelly to take Linton to the Heights. On the way, she does her best to reassure Linton about his father, even though he has never met him.

At Wuthering Heights, young Linton gets a harsh welcome. Heathcliff curses his mother Isabella, then shouts at Linton when he does not want to eat his breakfast.

Linton clings desperately to Nelly as she is about to leave. Despite this, Nelly has no choice but to ride back to the Grange.

Nelly doesn't see Linton, but Heathcliff's housekeeper tells her that he remains weak.

When young Catherine is sixteen, she and Nelly go bird-watching on the moors. Nelly finds it hard to keep up as Catherine races ahead.

1. whining wretch: crybaby.

From afar, Nelly sees Catherine talking to two men. Coming closer, she sees it is Heathcliff and Hareton! Catherine recognises Hareton from their last meeting.

Heathcliff invites Catherine to Wuthering Heights to visit Linton. Nelly wonders what Heathcliff is up to.

Heathcliff tells Nelly he wants Catherine and Linton to marry. But when they meet, the two cousins barely recognise each other.

Linton's too feeble to show Catherine around, so she goes with Hareton. Linton is told to follow them.

Catherine stays all afternoon before returning home. The next day, she asks her father why he has kept Heathcliff and Hareton a secret.

But Catherine ignores her father. She writes to Linton in secret. Nelly finds his replies hidden in a drawer.

Nelly burns the letters, then sends a note to Linton telling him to stop writing to Catherine.

1. on any account: for any reason.
2. cordial: pleasant, nice.

HEATHCLIFF'S THREAT

Look! Winter's not here yet. There's a little flower up there.

Ho! Miss Linton!

As summer turns to autumn, Edgar becomes ill with a very bad cold. He spends less and less time with Catherine.

One November day, out on a walk with Nelly, Catherine climbs a wall and her hat falls to the other side.

Catherine climbs down to get it, but she can't climb back. Then she hears a deep voice behind her.

I swear Linton is dying. None but you can save him.

Hopefully one look at Linton will prove Heathcliff a liar.

It's Heathcliff. He scolds Catherine for not writing to Linton any more. He asks her to pay a visit while he is away.

Catherine pesters Nelly to take her back to Wuthering Heights. Nelly reluctantly agrees.

The following morning, Catherine and Nelly ride to Wuthering Heights. Soon Linton and Catherine get into an argument about their fathers.

My papa scorns[1] yours. He calls him a sneaking fool.

Yours is a wicked man. He must be, to make Aunt Isabella leave him.

In a rage, Catherine shoves Linton's chair.

You spiteful, cruel thing.

Linton has a coughing fit and accuses Catherine of attacking him.

1. scorns: looks down on.

Suddenly, Linton falls to the floor. Catherine helps him up. Feeling guilty, she tends to him.

On the way home, Nelly catches a cold. Catherine nurses Edgar and Nelly during the day, but looks after Linton at night. Nelly catches her, and Catherine reveals all.

Where is she going at this hour?

Miss Catherine, I can read now.

Catherine describes how on one of her visits, Hareton read out his name above the door.

What about the date?

I can't read numbers yet.

You dunce![1]

When Catherine laughs at Hareton for being stupid, he takes out his anger on Linton.

Get to thy[2] own room!

Hareton's attack gives Linton a coughing fit: blood gushes from his mouth and he falls to the ground.

Sobbing in fury, Catherine whips Hareton. She heads for home.

I'm ill because of you, Catherine.

When Catherine returns a few days later, Linton blames her for his coughing fit.

I am worthless, but your kindness has made me love you deeper.

Fed up with Linton, Catherine tries to say goodbye, but he just bursts into tears.

You went behind my back, Catherine.

Nelly repeats to Edgar everything she hears from Catherine. Edgar bans his daughter from visiting Wuthering Heights, but will allow Linton to come to the Grange.

1. dunce: stupid person.
2. thy: your.

33

IMPRISONED!

Nelly stops her story to ask Mr Lockwood what he thinks of Catherine.

Lockwood urges Nelly to carry on with the story. She explains that Catherine does stop visiting Linton, but Linton never comes to the Grange.

Edgar, worried that he will soon die, wonders why Linton never visits. He also worries about his daughter.

Edgar would let her marry Linton if it made her happy, even if it meant Heathcliff got his hands on the Grange.

As he grows weaker, Edgar finally agrees to let Catherine meet Linton, not at Wuthering Heights, but on the moors that summer.

When Catherine and Nelly meet him, he is too weak to walk far from Wuthering Heights.

Linton insists he is better, panting and trembling all the time. As they talk, he keeps glancing back nervously at Wuthering Heights.

When they meet again a week later, Linton is more nervous than ever. Catherine asks him why he is acting so strangely.

1. How must I quit her?: How can I give her what is due to her?

"I cannot bear it. Leave me and I shall be killed."

"My father threatened me and I dread him."

Heathcliff has been forcing Linton to meet Catherine.

"The rumour goes that Edgar is on his death bed. How long will he last?"

Catherine hears a noise and sees Heathcliff approaching. At first he seems very friendly.

"I can't go to Wuthering Heights. Papa has forbidden me."

Heathcliff insists they all walk back to Wuthering Heights, despite Catherine's protests. Linton clings to Catherine as they walk.

"Stand off, or I shall knock you down!"

Once inside the house, Heathcliff locks them in. Catherine tries to grab the key from him, but fails.

"You must obey my father, you must!"

Heathcliff refuses to let them go until Catherine marries Linton. When he leaves the room, Linton persuades Catherine to agree.

"Take it!"

"Nay![1]"

"Stay one minute."

Catherine is allowed to leave the bedroom in which they are locked, but Nelly is imprisoned for five days, guarded and fed by Hareton.

"Is Catherine gone?"

"She's not to go..."

"...we won't let her."

On the fifth morning, Heathcliff's housekeeper, Zillah, frees Nelly. Nelly searches through the house until she finds Linton. He tells her that Catherine is upstairs – and that they are married.

"She's my wife now, but I'll not stay with her. She cries so I can't bear it."

"You're a heartless, selfish boy."

1. nay: no.

DIGGING UP THE DEAD

Catherine is alive and well, and will be here, I hope, tonight.

Heathcliff must be stopped!

Go away! Catherine is too ill to leave her room!

Before Heathcliff finds out, Nelly runs back to the Grange. She is shocked by the change in Edgar, who appears close to death.

Edgar sends for his lawyer, planning to change his will to stop the Grange going into Heathcliff's hands.

Nelly sends a group of men to rescue Catherine, but Heathcliff blocks them. Linton, however, takes pity on her and lets her go.

I am going to Cathy...

No more runnings away. I'm come to fetch you home.

Catherine rushes to her father's side. To allow him to die in peace, she lies that she is happily married to Linton. Edgar dies in her arms.

The lawyer arrives, dismissing all but Nelly, who persuades him to bury Edgar next to Cathy.

Shortly after the funeral, Heathcliff appears at the Grange to take Catherine back to Wuthering Heights.

I know Linton loves me and for that reason I love him. Mr Heathcliff, you have nobody to love you.

We shall have the revenge of knowing that your cruelty arises from your greater misery!

I'll tell you what I did yesterday!

While Catherine packs, Heathcliff begins to tell Nelly a shocking story.

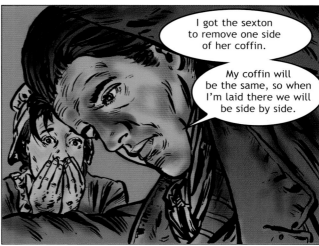

Heathcliff says he has always felt Cathy's ghost close by, whether out on the moors or in her room in Wuthering Heights.

As Catherine is about to set off with Heathcliff, she asks Nelly to visit her soon, but Heathcliff bans Nelly from coming to Wuthering Heights. Reluctantly, Catherine leaves with Heathcliff.

1. sexton: a person who looks after a church, often a bellringer as well as a gravedigger.
2. it is hers yet: though Catherine has been buried many years, Heathcliff can still recognise her face.
3. prying: snooping.

Linton Dies

Nelly tells Lockwood she still gets news of Catherine from Zillah – it seems Heathcliff has made life hell for his young daughter-in-law.

Despite this, Catherine nurses poor Linton alone until the day he dies. Heathcliff appears too late to say goodbye to his son.

Nelly tells Lockwood that she now has her own cottage. She wants Catherine to live with her, but knows Heathcliff will never allow it.

Nelly has come to the end of her story. By now Lockwood has fully recovered from his illness.

Lockwood goes to the Heights to tell Heathcliff that he will soon leave Thrushcross Grange – he can't bear to spend another winter there.

Lockwood travels again to the Yorkshire moors, to visit a friend. Learning that Nelly has moved back to Wuthering Heights, Lockwood rides to the manor. He notices that everything looks different.

Lockwood finds Nelly sewing and singing in the kitchen. She tells Lockwood that when Zillah left, Heathcliff gave her the job of housekeeper.

1. no remedy: no way out.

Nelly informs Lockwood that Heathcliff died three months before. She tells him all that has happened since he left Thrushcross Grange.

In the past months, Catherine, growing restless, has admitted to Nelly that she feels bad for laughing at Hareton because he can't read.

One day, Hareton was injured while out shooting. He spent the next few days in the kitchen recovering. At first, he and Catherine quarrelled.

Hareton accused her of treating him more like a servant than her cousin. But when Catherine stepped forward and gave him a gentle kiss on the cheek, Hareton didn't know what to say.

To show her goodwill, Catherine gave Hareton a book wrapped in white paper with his name written on it. She promised to teach him to read.

Later, Catherine and Hareton were seen seated on a bench with her hand on his shoulder. But it was just the beginning. Catherine and Hareton soon fell in love.

1. you are my cousin, and you shall own me: You are my cousin, and you should recognise that fact.
2. naught: nothing.
3. mucky pride: Hareton is saying that she is proud for no good reason, hence her pride is stained or 'mucky'.
4. mocking tricks: tricks Cathy plays to put Hareton down.

PEACE AT LAST

When Heathcliff found out that Hareton had been planting flowers for Catherine as a sign of their new friendship, he was furious. For once, Hareton just scoffed at him, while Cathy accused him of stealing all her land.

Heathcliff grabbed Catherine's hair roughly and was about to hit her when he stopped. Something in her eyes reminded him of her mother, Cathy.

Nelly tells Lockwood that a change soon came over Heathcliff. He didn't even want to punish Catherine and Hareton any more.

Heathcliff spent more and more time on his own and avoided meals with the rest of the house.

One day, Heathcliff spent the entire night out rambling, and when he returned he had a strange look in his eyes.

When Nelly begged him to come to dinner that night, he asked to be left alone. Nelly feared he was ill.

That evening, as Nelly went round shutting the windows, her candle suddenly lit up Heathcliff's face. She was terrified by his black, staring eyes and ghostly white face. Heathcliff was staring into space as if someone – or something – was there.

Heathcliff seemed to be talking to a ghost. Nelly could see nothing. In the following days, Heathcliff became increasingly odd. He kept muttering Cathy's name out loud.

A couple of days later, Nelly went to find Heathcliff. Peeping into his bedroom, she saw him staring and smiling at her.

Moving closer, she saw that he was not resting – he was dead. In death he could finally be with his darling Cathy again.

Nelly tells Lockwood that Hareton and Catherine are to marry. But when the loving couple arrive, Lockwood feels it is time to leave.

Lockwood walks across the moors to the churchyard. He finds the graves of Edgar, Cathy and Heathcliff.

The End 41

EMILY BRONTË (1818-1848)

Though the power and drama of her one novel *Wuthering Heights* (1847) made Emily Brontë famous after her death, very little is known about her life. None of the letters she left behind reveal much about her personality and, unlike her sisters Charlotte and Anne, she seems to have put little of herself into her book.

From what we do know about her, Emily was a quiet, painfully shy person who was just as happy spending time with the family pets as with people. Yet she was also strong-willed and fearless – in one story, after she was bitten by a rabid dog, she cleaned the wound herself using a hot iron.

Emily Brontë, as painted by her brother, Branwell.

EMILY'S PARENTS

Her father was born Patric Prunty (1777–1861) in County Down, Ireland. Despite being the son of a humble storyteller, he won a place at Cambridge University. Around 1799, he changed his name to the more impressive-sounding Brontë. After leaving Cambridge, Patric Brontë became a Church of England clergyman and married a Cornish woman, Marie Branwell, in 1812.

Emily, born on 30 July 1818, was the fifth of their six children. In 1820, the family moved to Haworth in Yorkshire (now West Yorkshire). Her father remained as curate for the rest of his life.

SCHOOLDAYS

After Marie died in September 1821, her unmarried sister Elizabeth Branwell came to look after the children. She brought the children up according to strict Methodist principles, and the menacing, grumpy character of the servant Joseph in *Wuthering Heights* may be based on her.

In 1824, the girls were sent to attend the Clergy Daughters' School at nearby Cowan Bridge. The girls were treated so badly there that Emily's elder sisters Maria and Elizabeth both became ill with tuberculosis and died shortly after they returned home. For the next few years the children were educated at home. They were left very much to themselves and spent their days roaming the nearby moors or making up stories.

In 1826, Emily's younger brother Branwell got a box of wooden toy soldiers as a present. The children gave each soldier a name and invented a fantasy kingdom in Africa where these characters lived.

LIFE AS A SCHOOLTEACHER

In 1835, Emily's elder sister Charlotte became a teacher at Miss Wooler's School in Roe Head, not many miles from Haworth. Emily, who was now 17, joined her as a pupil but became so homesick that she starved herself and returned home just three months later. There were few jobs for poor curate's daughters in those days, so Emily started work as a teacher near Halifax in 1838. The job was exhausting and Emily hated it. Within six months, she was home again.

Charlotte had a plan to set up their own school, so she and Emily went to Brussels in February 1842 to study the languages that would help make their school a success.

However, when their aunt died later that year, they returned to Haworth for the funeral and never left again. When their plan to open a school failed, Emily resigned herself to a life of looking after her father and their family home.

POEMS AND NOVELS

In 1845, Charlotte, Anne and Emily found out they had all been writing poetry. Within a year, they had published a collection of the poems under the pen names Currer, Ellis and Acton Bell, using the money left to them by their dead Aunt Elizabeth. Their publishing venture was a disaster. Though it cost them £50 (more than a year's wages for most workers) to print the books, they only sold two copies!

Undaunted, the sisters then decided to write a novel each. By the winter of 1847, Emily's *Wuthering Heights*, Anne's *Agnes Grey* and Charlotte's *Jane Eyre* were published. Though *Jane Eyre* was an immediate success, critics and the public at first ignored *Wuthering Heights* and *Agnes Grey*.

DEATH

Less than a year later, in September 1848, Emily's brother Branwell died. At the funeral, Emily caught a cold which developed into tuberculosis. Though Emily found it hard to breathe and was in great pain, she refused to see a doctor until it was too late.

She died on 19 December 1848 and was buried three days later in the family vault at Haworth.

SPOT THE MISTAKE

Wuthering Heights was Emily Brontë's first and only novel. She and her sisters only set out to write a novel each after they failed to sell their published collected poems. However, when her sister Charlotte's novel *Jane Eyre* became an instant hit, her publisher Thomas Cautley Newby rushed the books by Emily and Anne into print to cash in on its success. In fact, he did it so quickly he didn't bother to check for spelling mistakes, so the first edition of *Wuthering Heights* is full of errors!

BRONTË'S INFLUENCES

People once believed that Emily wrote the book alone, cut off from the outside world. However, though she was very shy, Brontë had studied the works of classic writers in her father's library and while in Brussels – she even taught herself German to read works by German Romantic writers. Brontë was also a fan of the poetry of Lord Byron, and it is possible that the relationship between Heathcliff and Cathy was influenced by one of Byron's poems. The bleak Yorkshire Moors near Emily's home of Haworth did

LINTON/EARNSHAW FAMILY TREE

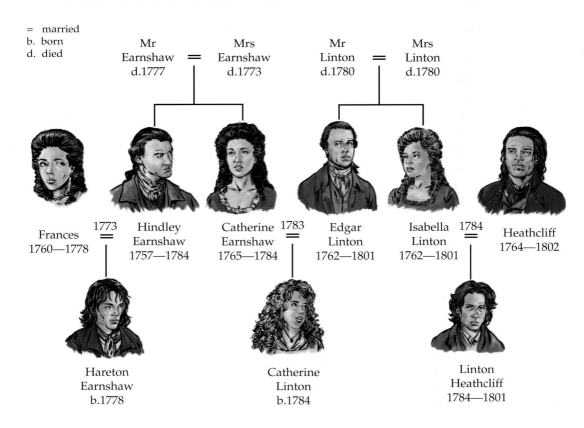

= married
b. born
d. died

| Mr Earnshaw d.1777 | = | Mrs Earnshaw d.1773 | | Mr Linton d.1780 | = | Mrs Linton d.1780 |

Frances 1760—1778 = 1773 Hindley Earnshaw 1757—1784

Catherine Earnshaw 1765—1784 = 1783 Edgar Linton 1762—1801

Isabella Linton 1762—1801 = 1784 Heathcliff 1764—1802

Hareton Earnshaw b.1778

Catherine Linton b.1784

Linton Heathcliff 1784—1801

influence the book in other ways. When Brontë was away from the moors, she missed them terribly – just like Cathy. The wild, stormy landscape gives the book its moody atmosphere and mirrors the violent moods of many of the characters.

On a misty night, the moors are a spooky place and it is no wonder that Brontë imagined the ghosts and visions that haunted Heathcliff. She was also influenced by the Gothic novels of the 18th century, such as Mary Shelley's famous *Frankenstein*, which have the same gloomy atmosphere.

The bleak and blustery Yorkshire Moors play a major role in Wuthering Heights.

WHY ELLIS BELL?

The book was first published in December 1847, under the name Ellis Bell. *Wuthering Heights* was not the sort of book that Victorian women were supposed to write, so Brontë used a male name. At first, the novel was attacked by critics, who thought the characters were too horrific and cruel – some even said the author must be mad! Even Emily's sister Charlotte was unhappy with some of the darker moments in the book. Other critics were confused by the original and complicated way in which the story is told, with several flashbacks and the main story of the Earnshaw and Linton families being told by two narrators, Nelly and Mr Lockwood.

Wuthering Heights also attacks the world in which Brontë lived, where women were expected to be gentle, meek and interested only in romance and fashion. Her heroines are strong-willed and wild – they prefer riding across the windswept moors to a quiet life at home. Brontë lived at a time when most people were very religious and one was expected to behave properly. Yet surprisingly, she leaves it up to the reader to decide for themselves whether Heathcliff is right to behave in the way he does.

Like most writers, Brontë was influenced by events in her own family. The drunken Hindley is perhaps partly based on watching her brother Branwell drink himself to death at an early age.

SUCCESS AT LAST

In 1850, two years after Emily died, Charlotte published a second edition of *Wuthering Heights*. This time, the book was a critical and commercial success, and by the end of the 19th century it was regarded as one of the greatest novels ever written.

TIMELINE OF EMILY BRONTË

There were many important events that occurred during the lifetime of Emily Brontë – many of which marked a changing world. Emily's views on women were equally forward-thinking and important for their time.

30 July 1818
Emily Brontë is born in Thornton, Yorkshire, England.

1819
Simón Bolívar liberates New Granada (now Colombia, Venezuela and Ecuador) from Spain.

First steamship crosses the Atlantic Ocean.

The United States buys Florida from Spain.

1821
Michael Faraday invents the first electric motor.

John Constable paints *The Hay Wain*.

Emily Brontë's mother dies.

1822
Greece declares independence from Turkey.

1824
Beethoven's Ninth Symphony is first performed.

1825
First passenger-carrying railway in England.

1826
Oldest surviving photograph taken by Joseph-Nicéphore Niepce (France).

1830
John Matthews invents machine for making soft (fizzy) drinks.

1832
English Parliament passes the First Reform Act, so that industrial cities such as Manchester and Birmingham can elect members of parliament for the first time.

1833
Slavery is abolished in the British Empire.

1834
Charles Babbage invents the mechanical adding machine, a forerunner of computers.

1835
James Bowman Lindsay invents the first electric lightbulb.

1836
Boer farmers start the 'Great Trek', founding republics in Natal, Transvaal and Orange Free State in South Africa.

1837
Charles Dickens publishes the final instalment of *The Pickwick Papers*, his first novel.

Queen Victoria is crowned.

1844
Samuel F. B. Morse invents the telegraph machine.

1845
Emily Brontë begins *Wuthering Heights*.

1846
US declares war on Mexico – the war lasts until 1849.

1847
Wuthering Heights is published.

Jane Eyre, written by Charlotte Brontë under the pen name Currer Bell, is published.

1848
Revolutions across Europe. Most are put down by royal troops, but in France, Louis Napoleon is elected president of the French Republic.

The Tenant of Wildfell Hall, written by Anne Brontë under the pen name Acton Bell, is published.

19 December: Emily Brontë dies from tuberculosis.

1850
The second edition of *Wuthering Heights* is published, this time to great critical acclaim and commercial success.

With its dramatic story and brooding landscapes, it's no surprise that Emily Brontë's *Wuthering Heights* has been made into several movies and been adapted for TV and radio many times. It has also inspired a musical by Bernard J. Taylor, the hit pop song *Wuthering Heights* written and performed by Kate Bush (which went to No. 1 in the UK charts in 1978), and even a ballet and opera.

The first film version of the story was a silent movie made in 1920 by director A. V. Bramble. Sadly, as no prints of the film survive, no-one knows how the story was handled in the days before sound.

The most famous adaptation for the silver screen was made in 1939, starring Laurence Olivier as Heathcliff, Merle Oberon as Cathy, and David Niven as Edgar Linton. The movie was a great love story and a wonderful film – it was nominated for an Academy Award for Best Picture – but it left out half of the book and set the story 150 years later than the original.

Bernard Herrmann wrote an opera based on the novel in 1951, and in 1995 the story was adapted for the stage by the English playwright Gillian Hiscott.

TV adaptations were made of the book in 1970 and 1978. These were much more faithful to the original story, unlike the movie made in 1992 which starred Ralph Fiennes as Heathcliff and Juliette Binoche as both Cathy and her daughter, Catherine Linton. In this version, the farmhouse at Wuthering Heights looks more like a gothic mansion from a spooky horror movie!

In the past twenty years, the book has also been filmed in Arabic, French, German, Japanese and Filipino – perfectly illustrating what a wide and international appeal the book has round the globe.

OTHER WORKS BY EMILY BRONTË

1846
Emily's first published work was the book *Poems by Currer, Ellis and Acton Bell*, which she published with her sisters Charlotte and Anne in 1846 with their own money – but the book sold only two copies.

1847
Emily published her first and only novel, *Wuthering Heights*, under the pseudonym (pen name) of Ellis Bell.

1848
Emily's publisher T. C. Newby sent her a letter dated 15 February which talked to her about her next (second) novel. Sadly, Emily died before she had finished it.

INDEX

IF YOU LIKED THIS BOOK, YOU MIGHT LIKE TO TRY THESE OTHER GRAFFEX TITLES:

Jane Eyre Charlotte Brontë

Julius Caesar William Shakespeare

Hamlet William Shakespeare

Treasure Island Robert Louis Stevenson

Oliver Twist Charles Dickens

Moby-Dick Herman Melville

The Hunchback of Notre Dame Victor Hugo

Kidnapped Robert Louis Stevenson

Journey to the Centre of the Earth Jules Verne

Dracula Bram Stoker

The Man in the Iron Mask Alexandre Dumas

Frankenstein Mary Shelley

Macbeth William Shakespeare

The Three Musketeers Alexandre Dumas

A Tale of Two Cities Charles Dickens

Adventures of Huckleberry Finn Mark Twain

Dr Jekyll and Mr Hyde Robert Louis Stevenson